BANDELIER
NATIONAL MONUMENT

WRITTEN BY
PATRICIA BAREY

PHOTOGRAPHS BY
GEORGE H. H. HUEY

WESTERN NATIONAL PARKS ASSOCIATION
TUCSON, ARIZONA

COVER—Long House

TITLE PAGE—Tsankawi Black-on-Cream vessel

THIS PAGE AND FACING PAGE—The Large Kiva, drawing by R.P. McClung, 1939

Copyright 1990 by Western National Parks Association
Tucson, Arizona
Library of Congress Number 90-060724
ISBN 978-091140888-1
Author-Patricia Barey
Artifact descriptions-Rory Gauthier
Editorial- T. J. Priehs, Therese Burson, Chris Judson, Cecelia Shields, Sally King
Book design-Christina Watkins
Typography- TypeWorks
Lithography-Sung In.
Printed in Korea

Design element adapted from Tsankawi ceramic depicts the Awanyu, or feathered serpent, which is symbolic of water to pueblo peoples.

ACKNOWLEDGMENTS–We think of writing as a solitary craft and so it is much of the time. But on a project like this, long before a writer confronts the blank page or computer screen, there are many people who give generously of their time, knowledge, and experience. I want to thank them because without them the task would be infinitely more difficult and not nearly as much fun.

The NPS staff at Bandelier, especially Ed Greene, Virginia Salazar, Rory Gauthier, Craig Allen, Andrea Sharon, Chris Judson, Cecelia Shields, and Sally King.

Therese Burson, whose fine sense of good writing helped capture the spirit of the place.

Peggy Hughes, who patiently and honestly read and re-read draft after draft.

Christina Watkins and George H. H. Huey, whose vision of the place helped me see it.

Tim Priehs at Western National Parks Association for giving me the chance to work on such an extraordinary project.

West Entrance

Contents

Cavate dwellings

Scarlet gilia

(OPPOSITE) **Cliff dwellings in Frijoles Canyon seen from the Long Trail**

CANYONS AND MESAS

In the high, dusty brown desert of north central New Mexico, the Jemez Mountains rise toward the sky. Within them lies the sprawling Pajarito Plateau where the air is thin and fragrant with pine and juniper and clear streams run even in the dry months. In a bright, blue sky, eagle wings pump, spread and take the wind, gliding in wide, silent arcs above the vast wilderness of Bandelier National Monument.

Bandelier is a maze of towering canyon walls and flat mesas in delicate shades of pink and buff. Downcanyon from the visitor center, the bubbling creek flows into the Rio Grande as it passes through the ancient rift that bears the river's name.

People have felt the pull of Bandelier's abundant resources for more than ten thousand years. Evidence of human habitation can be distinguished in the shapes of ancient structures now mounded with soil. Literally thousands of archeological sites have been identified, although fewer than fifty in the park have been excavated.

The stone rooms and silent kivas bear eloquent witness to thriving communities, but Bandelier was not always a verdant sanctuary in the desert. Its tranquil beauty, gentle streams, and pine-covered slopes belie a violent past. Millions of years ago, the earth beneath Bandelier trembled; it was the beginning of powerful geologic events that would dramatically re-shape the face of the land.

MOUNTAINS OF FIRE

The Rio Grande, great river of the Southwest, threads its peaceful way through the canyon and mesa country of north-central New Mexico. The shimmering green line bisecting the landscape two and a half miles southeast of Bandelier National Monument's park headquarters has determined the way of life here for centuries. But geologists reckon its history not in hundreds, but in millions of years. To them, the river marks the Rio Grande Rift, one of the largest rift valleys in the world, and one of the Southwest's most important geologic features.

This giant fissure in the earth's surface, running from central Colorado to northern Mexico, was caused by tensions that built up deep within the earth some thirty million years ago, forcing the crust to pull apart. Faulting—the opposite of the compression and corrugating effect that lifted the Rocky Mountains sixty-five million years ago—created fissures in the face of the earth all along the rift, like cracks in fine old china.

The rolling back of the crustal plates was accompanied by earthquakes and eruptions as newly opened vents permitted the release of steam, boiling ash, and rock from the hot magma layer below. Periods of relative calm probably alternated with violent explosions along the rift as the earth restlessly rearranged itself.

An artist's conception of the geology of the region

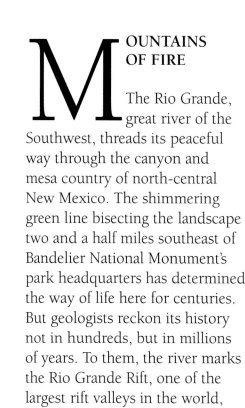

JEMEZ VOLCANIC FIELD

VALLES CALDERA

BANDELIER NATIONAL MONUMENT

RIO GRANDE

Cerros del Rio Flow

CERROS DEL RIO

Santa Fe

From the edge of mesas west of the Rio Grande near Los Alamos, the view reveals startlingly different landscapes caused by distinct geologic events on the two sides of the rift.

South and east of the river valley stand the cinder cone vents of the Cerros del Rio. This group of volcanoes, part of the larger Jemez volcanic field, rumbled ominously four million years ago, then shot hot gases and molten lava high into the air. When the explosive lava bursts hit the atmosphere, they solidified and fell as igneous rock and glowing ash around the vents. Even after centuries of erosion, these mountains retain cinder cone shapes. Wave after wave of lava surged from these cones, filling valleys and creek beds for many miles on both sides of the rift before it hardened into basalt, a dense, hard, black rock.

Today in Bandelier National Monument, the basalt layers, pocked with gas bubbles and shiny, green olivine crystals, form the base of the canyon walls along the Falls Trail, which follows El Rito de los Frijoles (Little River of the Beans).

About 13 million years ago, another seething volcanic area released its pent-up fury on the west side of the rift. Two climactic outbursts occurred 1.6 and 1.2 million years ago—the ash produced was 600 times the volume of the 1980 eruption of Washington State's Mt. St. Helens.

The magma from these eruptions was different in character: rich in silica, it was stiff and pasty. The gases trapped in it were unable to escape easily, and so its release was much more violent. Towering clouds of gases, volcanic dust, ash, and cinders obscured the sun and rained dust as far away as what is now Texas, Nebraska, and Iowa. The ash mixture roared down the mountainsides at hurricane speeds up to 100 miles an hour, and changed the face of the earth over 400 square miles. It settled over the older basalt from the Cerros del Rio

View of the Cerros del Rio from the Pajarito Plateau

explosions, encasing this rock layer to a depth of 1,000 feet in some places, and forming a uniformly flat, sloping plateau. An archeologist later translated a Tewa place name, "Little Bird," to Spanish, calling it the Pajarito Plateau.

The ash, which had fallen everywhere like dark rain, was transformed as it cooled. It welded together as tuff, a rock much lighter and softer than basalt. Tuff forms the distinctive pink, beige, and white cliffs that delight visitors to Bandelier.

The outer edges of the tuff cooled quickly as they met the cool ground and the atmosphere, while inner layers may have taken many years to harden and fuse together. Over time, erosion created the sponge-like pockets that give the cliff face its distinctive appearance today. Early peoples would discover this difference in the hardness of the rock and, with simple hand tools, carve homesites into the friable tuff.

As the magma was released from the vents, the volcanoes collapsed of their own weight, leaving a nearly circular depression or caldera. The Valles Caldera—what remains of the exhausted Jemez volcanoes—is just a short drive a few miles northwest of Bandelier National Monument.

Following State Route 4, north from Bandelier toward Jemez Springs, the road winds up the side and over the rim of the caldera before it suddenly emerges into a clearing. There, in the brilliant mountain sunlight, lies a broad, grassy meadow, a breathtaking six-mile-wide sea of tranquility the Spanish called Valle Grande. In its entirety, the Valles Caldera is one of the world's largest such geologic features, stretching roughly sixteen miles across.

After the collapse, the caldera filled with water, forming a lake considerably wider than Oregon's famed Crater Lake. On the slopes outside the caldera, rain and snowmelt etched ravines and finger-like canyons as they sought out the land's lowest level, the bed of the Rio Grande. These streams met little resistance from the soft layers of tuff. Eventually the lake itself drained.

In time, mountain streams like Frijoles Creek knifed through the soft volcanic tuff and down to the hard basalt. In some places the tuff has eroded about 1,000 feet in the million years since the volcanoes became extinct, a very fast pace in geologic time. The hard basalt offers a stiffer challenge. Along the Falls Trail, where Frijoles Creek plunges over steep falls before it joins the Rio Grande in spectacular White Rock Canyon, the creek has already cut almost 200 feet into the basalt.

Bandelier's violent past prompts the inevitable question: "Will the volcanoes erupt

For at least 10,000 years, obsidian deposits in the Jemez Mountains and within Bandelier National Monument were used by early peoples to make cutting or piercing tools like this obsidian biface. A naturally occurring volcanic glass, obsidian was highly prized because it was easy to work and had an extremely sharp edge. During the ancestral Pueblo culture, obsidian became an important trade item with groups as far as Texas and Oklahoma.

(OPPOSITE) **Lower Falls in Frijoles Canyon**

again?" If you consider geologic time, the answer is probably "Yes." Hot springs in the Jemez Mountains and earthquake tremors along the rift indicate continued geologic activity. The Jemez volcano is dormant, not extinct. There is evidence of plastic magma below. But in terms of human history, it is unlikely we will see Bandelier retreat again into the shadows of smoke and ash.

Evening primrose

Valley Grande in the Valles Caldera

The early people of Bandelier fashioned stone into a variety of tools including knives, dart points, and arrow points. Obsidian was the most popular material for making tools but they also used locally available basalt, chert, chalcedony, and quartzite. These tools include (from left to right) an obsidian arrowpoint dating to the Basketmaker III period, a small arrowpoint made of quartzite, and an Archaic dart point made from basalt.

PEOPLE OF THE PAJARITO PLATEAU

When the volcanic fires had long been extinguished, a cooler, wetter time descended over the Pajarito Plateau. The sun's rays pierced the mists only intermittently as the last Ice Age, the Pleistocene, waned on the American continent. After the distant glaciers retreated northward, the silence of centuries on the high plateau, now deeply carved by time and weather, was finally broken by the first human voices.

The earliest Southwest peoples identified by archeologists traversed the landscape in pursuit of large mammals now extinct: mammoths, long-haired bison, and camel-like creatures that roamed the region ten thousand years ago. The hunters made ragged-edged projectile points, today called "Clovis" and "Folsom" points after the places in New Mexico where this early evidence of human activity was discovered. These points were finely crafted, perhaps the finest ever made in the Americas. The highly effective spear points ripped through hide and flesh after the hunters had cornered their prey in narrow canyons or herded them to the edge of the high cliffs where they fell to their deaths.

The small human bands—no more than extended family groups—could rest from their wanderings beside mountain streams where there was an abundance of sweet wild plums and chokecherries. When they had eaten their fill and loaded what they could carry, the hunt resumed. Perhaps, memory of wild berries, plentiful nuts, and the warmth of the summer sun stored in high cliff walls lured them back another autumn.

By 5500 BCE (Before Common Era), a date considered the most ancient limit of the Archaic Period in Southwest archeology, the cycle of sunlight and moisture gradually shifted toward the sun-drenched climate, bright blue skies, and vegetation patterns that characterize life on the plateau today: Ponderosa pine forests prevailed at high elevations; juniper and piñon dominated at lower elevations while sage, saltbush, and cactus grew in the hotter canyon floors, much as they do today. Deer, elk, mountain lion, rabbit, porcupine, and squirrels wandered the land. Hawks and eagles climbed columns of air above the canyon floors.

The silence was broken more frequently now by people hunting small game and gathering wild food. Because a drier climate now prevailed, they roamed a wider area to survive; they did not yet stay on the plateau. Established communities did not develop until between 400 CE (Common era) and 1000 CE.

But proof of these earlier nomadic people in the vicinity of Bandelier was found during the 1977 excavation of Cochiti Reservoir. Many points along the river drainages revealed campsites typical of these early wanderers: shallow hearths accompanied by a scattering of fire-cracked rocks. They heated the rocks in the fire—usually quartzite or river cobbles—and then threw them, still glowing, into watertight, pitch-lined baskets to simmer a stew or parch seeds. After several heatings, the rocks split and were discarded near the hearths––telltale emblems of human subsistence.

These early hunters had developed a clever extension of the hunter's arm, the atlatl, a hooked throwing stick that they used to launch spears made with tips of obsidian found on the plateau. But it was their special skill at weaving yucca and other plant fibers into cooking, carrying, and storage baskets that became their identifying trademark.

Toward the end of the Archaic Period (600 CE), a new type of artifact signals the beginning of a major shift in lifestyle. Shallow stone basins that served as mortars and heavy grinding stones are found at campsites. They were used to crush wild seeds, nuts, and tubers and, eventually, to grind cultivated foods. These people were no longer constantly on the move in search of available food; they were inclined to stop, at least seasonally, in one place.

These early farmers were growing a type of small-eared corn developed in southern Mexico, along with beans and several varieties of squash, to supplement their hunting and gathering. Middens excavated near these pit-house settlements reveal a rich diet of gathered and cultivated foods: small animals, wild amaranth, mustard and sunflower seeds, corn, squash, and pumpkins.

Gradual adaptation to a sedentary, agricultural way of life continued for another six hundred years during the time archeologists designate as the Developmental Period of

Cane cholla

groups in this area. The people continued to make baskets but increasingly they favored pottery, for cooking.

The earliest pots were coarse, gray cooking vessels, but soon a white pot, decorated with black geometric designs—Kwahe'e black-on-white—appeared as evidenced by the sherds found abundantly in the upper Rio Grande River Valley. Tool kits expanded to include cultivating implements like scoops and digging sticks.

The shift from a nomadic hunting-and-gathering lifestyle to a settled one more suitable for farming demanded permanent shelters and places to store the fruits of their harvests. They began to build above ground with mud mortar and stone.

During the Coalition Period—from the 1100s to the 1300s—the people of the Southwest were growing in numbers and coming together. Living in larger groups, they could share the work of hunting and farming, and—no longer concerned merely with survival from one day to the next—they could make bigger plans. Communities traded ideas as well as material goods.

To the northwest of Bandelier National Monument, in the Four Corners area and in the San Juan River Basin, the ancestral Pueblo people increased and spread out. They became skilled farmers who designed ingenious water-control systems to irrigate neatly laid out

fields, a skill essential to survival in this desert landscape. Excelling at the stone mason's art, they built the amazing cliff dwellings of Mesa Verde, Betatakin, Keet Seel, and the great stone pueblos at Chaco Canyon.

Nothing in the decades prior to 1100 CE seems to foretell this great creative burst of the ancestral Pueblo culture. It is clear that the achievements of the ancestral Pueblos in farming technology, stone masonry, trade, and communication required a highly organized society. The cooperative effort necessary for this remarkable period of relative peace and prosperity was probably rooted in complex religious ritual. Most archeologists think these religious activities were centered in the great kivas, large underground ceremonial rooms.

About the year 1200 CE, an extended period of drought undermined the always-fragile balance of life in the Southwest. Although the exact reason people

One of the earliest pottery styles made in the Bandelier area, Santa Fe Black-on-White is believed to have derived from pottery styles popular in the San Juan Basin and Mesa Verde areas. The unusual shape of this miniature vessel suggests it was used for something out of the ordinary. The small handles indicated that it may have been suspended by leather straps or cord.

(OPPOSITE) Frijoles Canyon

Desert cottontail

moved away from the great stone pueblos such as those at Chaco Canyon remains unknown, the ancestral Pueblo people were probably forced to leave their homes because they could no longer support themselves with the fruits of their drought-withered fields. The canyon

vacated, the population of the Rio Grande River Valley was growing rapidly. It seems fairly certain that refugees from the drought-stricken north joined the already thriving and still relatively mobile plateau communities.

Life on the Pajarito Plateau was expanding as people migrated to the area. Families built one-room mud-and-brush shelters near small garden plots. Often three or four related family groups banded together, living in single-story block homes made of mud and stone. Each house had about eight surface rooms and an underground kiva. Three to five rooms provided living space with the other rooms used for storage. Sometimes households combined in fifteen- to twenty-room enclaves having one or two kivas. Hundreds of these small, neatly constructed homesites have been found in the ponderosa pine and piñon forest areas of the plateau.

Dwellings carved from volcanic tuff

dwellers, as well as those in the dozens of outlying villages, scattered.

For those who found their way a hundred miles to the south, the landscape of the Pajarito Plateau around Bandelier must have seemed like an oasis. Protected somewhat by the Jemez Mountains, the eastward-facing hamlets on the plateau and in Frijoles Canyon escaped the worst of the ravaging drought.

About the time the large pueblos to the north were

The village ceremonial life probably did not extend beyond these family enclaves; they performed rituals to maintain family harmony and supplicate spirits for favorable growing conditions. The large number of homesites suggests that the people continued to move frequently.

As people began to migrate from the north, the south, and the west, they were greeted by people who had already lived in this area for some time. Immigrants found precious resources such as a stable water supply, plants, and animals. Cliff dwellers and stonemasons would have been attracted to the plateau area by the dominant feature of the Bandelier landscape, its unique and abundant stone. From the towering pink and white cliffs formed from soft volcanic tuff, down to the hard black basalt, layer upon layer of mineral-rich rock offered these people an important resource.

In the Bandelier cliffs, cavities created by the ceaseless work of wind and water became shelters for the ancestral Pueblo people. The earliest hunters and foragers on the plateau

Tyuonyi

probably took advantage of the shallow, cave-like openings at the base of the cliffs. These natural caves offered protection from the sun, wind, and rain. In the thirteenth century the settlers discovered that the soft tuff yielded easily to their stone tools. Beginning around 1300 CE, building on the plateau and in the canyon began in earnest.

During the next century there was a gradual movement from the homesites at higher elevations down to more protected sites in the bottom of Frijoles Canyon. Pueblos built of stone quarried from the cliffs grew in size.

A typical pueblo from this period is the graceful Tyuonyi (pronounced Qu-weh-nee) located midway between Frijoles Creek and the north canyon face. Two and perhaps three stories high in some places, this village housed about one hundred people in four hundred rooms. It had three small kivas and a single ground-level entrance.

Tyuonyi's rooms must have been cramped and smoky, but its inhabitants spent most of their days working and playing in the central outdoor plaza. Kivas, like the large one to the east of the village, served as the center for village ceremonial life. The people entered this large underground chamber through an opening in the roof. They then

climbed down a ladder to a fire-lit room containing a hearth and rectangular hollows in the floor that may have served as foot drums. A small hole near the center of the floor symbolized the point of emergence of people into this world.

In this shadow-filled subterranean room, halfway between the spirit world below and the everyday world of human activity above, the ancestral Pueblo people would pray their world into harmony. Here they performed ceremonies that bound communities together and passed on cultural values to the young.

In addition to this freestanding pueblo on the canyon floor, this period also saw the construction of condominium-like pueblos against the north wall of the canyon. The most remarkable of these is Long House, which stretches for some eight hundred feet and consisted of two or three rows of rooms extending outward from the rock face. Holes that once held roof beams form neat rows in the cliff and clearly indicate the size of this multi-storied village.

Alongside these large pueblos, the people of the Pajarito Plateau continued to build the old-style small homesites and to follow their traditional pattern of moving frequently from one home to another. So, although several thousand sites have been located within Bandelier's boundaries, this alone is not a good indication of the area's population. Some sites with hearths scarcely blackened seem to have been occupied for only a year or two, a few for as little as six months.

Archeologists don't know for certain why the ancestral Puebloans moved so frequently. Some evidence suggests that large sites, with their rows of storage rooms and underground kivas, were winter homes while the small homesites provided shelter closer to the fields during the growing season. Perhaps the inhabitants of Bandelier simply liked a change of scenery. At any rate, the wide variety of game and wild and cultivated foods allowed for great mobility.

This period, from about 1300 CE to 1500 CE, saw a difference in building styles as well as sizes: the canyon-dwellers built both

Petroglyph of a turkey at Long House. The petroglyph design was modified for a logo by Bandelier lodge owner Evelyn Frey, and it has since become the logo of the park.

(OPPOSITE) Tyuonyi Pueblo in Frijoles Canyon

Cavate dwelling

free-standing masonry pueblos and cave dwellings carved from the cliffs. Some theorize that the ancestral Pueblo people were making use of solar energy. The carved-out rooms in Bandelier's north cliff walls face south, where they can absorb the thin rays of winter sun riding low on the southern horizon. The temperature on the cliff face can average thirteen degrees warmer than on the canyon floor.

Whatever the reasons for their flexible housing arrangements, the canyon-dwellers' many homesites have provided scholars with abundant clues to their life here. However, most family life took place not in these dark rooms, but outside on the rooftops. Fortunately, they neglected to clean these open spaces thoroughly.

They took what they valued and what they could carry and moved on. Later, the old roof often collapsed and the debris of daily life—broken pots, discarded tools and baskets, outworn clothing, and food remains—tumbled in a heap, creating rich refuse mounds for those who would have the patience to comb through them for answers.

In addition to their masonry building skills, the people of the Pajarito Plateau made many technological advances during this "Classic Phase" (1300 CE or 1325 to circa 1525 CE) of occupation, including the construction of small-scale irrigation channels to water their crops.

The ancestral people of the Pajarito Plateau developed a trail network that linked major pueblos in the canyon with those on top of the mesas. A sense of organization and purpose emanates from these narrow switchbacks that climb the cliffs —grooves deeply worn into the soft stone by generations of use.

Considerable cultural diversity existed on the Pajarito Plateau as people exchanged goods over a wide area. One intriguing discovery is a distinction that seemed to exist between settlers on the mesa north of Frijoles Canyon and those to the south. Artifacts from the northern sites suggest an unbroken line of continuity extending from the earliest coalition settlements in the 1100s through the period of peak population in the 1400s, until people moved away. Changes in technology, settlement, and social organization in the north appear to be an outgrowth of earlier methods of coping with the

Shaped by chipping, pecking, and grinding, stone axes such as this were used to cut trees for roof beams and firewood. The handle consists of a slender stick which was bent around the grooved axe head and secured with sinew or cord. This handle is a replica of an actual stone axe and wood handle found by archeologist surveying sites in the Bandelier backcountry.

(OPPOSITE) Footpath in a tuff at Tsankawi

plateau's environment. In Frijoles Canyon and to the south, several striking differences signal the possible presence of newcomers to the area: the appearance of Rio Grande glazeware pottery, different in size and shape from earlier carbon-painted vessels, and the presence of both very large and very small house sites indicating a more sophisticated and flexible community organization.

This prehistoric division roughly parallels the differences in modern pueblo life between the Tewa-speaking people who live on the northern plateau and upper Rio Grande Valley and the Keres-speaking people to the south, near Cochiti. If this distinction is an accurate one, the large pueblos in Frijoles Canyon would have occupied a key middle ground between the two groups that could offer many opportunities for cultural exchange and enrichment.

During the 1400s the canyon settlements bustled with activity: On the northern plateau, homesites were consolidated into five large villages: Tsankawi, Tsirege, Navawi, Otowi, and Puye. In Frijoles Canyon as many as five hundred people lived in the large villages of Tyuonyi and Long House and in smaller scattered sites along a 1.5-mile section of the canyon.

In his popular nineteenth century novel, **The Delight Makers**, Adolph Bandelier imagines how the canyon scene would have looked to those descending the narrow canyon trail six hundred years ago:

The cliffs themselves extended north . . . and east and west as far as the range of view permitted. . . Their base was enlivened by the bustle of those who dwelt in caves all along the foot of the imposing rock wall. Where today only vacant holes stare at the visitor. . . human eyes peered through. Other doors were closed by deer hides or robes. Sometimes a man, a woman or a child, would creep out of one of these openings, and climbing upward, disappear in the entrance of an upper tier of cave-dwellings. Others would descend the slope from the cliffs to the fields, while still others returned from the banks of the ditch or of the brook.

A hundred years after this imagined scene, certainly by the mid-1500s, even the largest pueblos lay empty: No catastrophic drought or major climate change accounts for it. The Spanish explorers had not yet found their way so far north. Why the ancestral Pueblo people left the high plateau and fertile canyon where they had thrived for over four hundred years remains a mystery: Some archeologists believe that intensive farming practices and an expanding population simply outstripped natural resources and, like their ancestors before them, the people of the Pajarito Plateau packed all they could carry and moved on to join

Talus House

distant relatives along the Rio Grande Valley.

About 1580, the Spaniards came with their sheep and horses, new strains of corn, beans, and squash, metal tools, and weapons to enforce their ways. They changed life in the Rio Grande Valley—and in all of New Mexico—forever.

But the newcomers, first Spaniards and then Americans, did not find their way into the maze of canyons at once. For another 200 years the sunlit stone villages, which for so long had echoed with laughter and voices in many different native tongues, fell silent. Still the vast mesas beckoned only scattered farmers, shepherds, miners, and occasional Pueblo pilgrims. Time, wind, and soil encased villages and kivas in shroud-like mounds.

REVELATIONS IN EMPTY ROOMS

About four o'clock on a brilliant October afternoon in 1880, a curious adventurer named Adolph Bandelier was guided into Frijoles Canyon. Three months earlier, the Swiss-born immigrant had been checking figures in his father's bank in Highland, Illinois, dreaming of discovery. He had spent the better part of his forty years preparing to take over the family business. But he was destined to follow his passionate interest in native cultures.

He was an unlikely adventurer. He had no formal training for the work before him, only years of reading and a fervent desire to learn more. The Archaeological Institute of America had given him funds, but little other support for his one-man expedition to the Southwest. As a student of indigenous cultures, he was a rank amateur and it showed. Only a few weeks after he arrived at Santo Domingo Pueblo near Santa Fe, his eagerness almost put an abrupt end to his contact with the Pueblo people he had come so far to study: Impatient and untutored in the subtleties of gathering sensitive information, he offended the village elders with his relentless questions. They retaliated by cutting off his food supply. He tired of smuggled watermelons

This bowl, done in a style called Agua Fria Glaze-on-Red, is an example of the earliest glaze-decorated pottery made in the Bandelier area. It utilized a lead-based glaze, which was mined in the Cerrillos area south of Santa Fe. Pottery of this style was popular in the area from Frijoles Cauyon in Bandelier south to Socorro, New Mexico, and was made from 1300 C.E. to 1700 C.E.

and impulsively set off on his own for nearby Cochiti Pueblo. There he began the journey that would change his life and the fate of the country he explored.

As Bandelier and his Cochiti guide, Juan Jose Montoya, began on foot the steep descent through thickly tangled vegetation into Frijoles Canyon, something in the pattern of sunlight and shadow on the rosy cliffs of late afternoon made his heart pound. That night before the campfire, as was his habit throughout a lifetime of travel and research, he recorded what he found in the waning hours of the autumn day:

The grandest thing I ever saw. A magnificent growth of pines, encina, alamos, and towering cliffs, of pumice or volcanic tuff, exceedingly friable. The cliffs are vertical on the north side and their bases are, for a length, as yet unknown to me, used as dwellings both from the inside and by inserting the roof poles for stories outside. It is of the highest interest.

Over the next few days, Bandelier wandered the canyon and nearby mesas with Juan Jose, feverishly sketching the dwellings and recording impressions. They measured the mounds and caves with a meter rod Bandelier would carry as a walking stick for the rest of his life. He collected everything: pieces of flint and obsidian, potsherds, and even bits of mud. He boxed them all and sent them triumphantly to his sponsors at the Archaeological Institute of America. Sitting in their New York City boardroom, the distinguished scholars examined these artifacts with some puzzlement. They did not yet appreciate Bandelier's find,

Frijoles Canyon

26

**Adolph and Fanny Bandelier
in Peru, 1890**

E. COURRETY, COURTESY OF PALACE OF THE GOVERNORS, MUSEUM OF NEW MEXICO, PHOTO ARCHIVES #9128

but he knew it was momentous: "I'm dirty, tired, but of best cheer. My life's work has at last begun," he wrote to his mentor, Lewis H. Morgan.

Bandelier did not excavate any of the sites in Frijoles Canyon. Always restless, he moved on, recording some 166 sites during the eighteen months he traveled New Mexico before he journeyed to Mexico, Bolivia, and Peru. He rarely stopped at any site for longer than two weeks. After the historic 1880 trip, Bandelier returned only four times to the place that would be named in his honor. On each visit, he traveled on foot, sometimes in unrelenting heat and sometimes in blinding snowstorms, and camped in the most primitive conditions.

On one trip he was accompanied by a new friend who shared his enthusiasm for the quest. Charles F. Lummis gladly traveled the Southwest at Bandelier's side and recorded his own impressions:

Naturally, among my dearest memories of our trampings together is that of the Rito, the Tyuonyi. It had never in any way been pictured before. We were the first students that ever explored it . . . What days those were! The weather was no friend of ours, nor of the cameras. We were wet and half-fed, and cold by night, even in the ancient, tiny caves. But the unforgettable glory of it all!

Before Bandelier died in 1914 at age seventy-four—blinded by cataracts but still working in

Spanish archives with his wife at his side—he produced a vast body of observations and documentation that laid the foundation for future scholarship in southwestern history, ethnology, and archeology. His novel about ancestral Pueblo life in Frijoles Canyon, *The Delight Makers*, in which he intended to "clothe sober facts in the garb of romance," conveyed his findings to a popular audience and helped stir public interest in the work of other researchers in southwestern archeology.

Many old, sepia-tone photographs show a large man in high leather boots, wide puttees, and dapper bow tie posing in front of archeological sites all over the Southwest. Edgar Lee Hewett was certainly the most important of the researchers drawn to the world Bandelier brought to light. A man of broad, humanistic interests, he, too, was intrigued by the winding footpaths of the Pajarito Plateau. Beginning in 1896, Hewett and his American Indian guides tirelessly hiked the countryside, mapping the territory and marking hundreds of sites. He was also a brilliant and unorthodox teacher who demanded great resourcefulness and stamina of his students.

One of Hewett's first disciples was Alfred Kidder, later a famed archeologist in his own right. As a student, Kidder responded to an advertisement tacked on a Harvard University bulletin board seeking researchers for work in the Southwest. After a cross-country train trip and a sixty-mile wagon ride, Kidder met the great Hewett who, on the following day, led his band of young helpers "miles down a blazing hot canyon," then to the top of a mesa. There they beheld a panoramic view of mesas and canyons stretching away to the horizon under a cloudless turquoise sky. "None of us had ever viewed so much of the world all at one time," Kidder wrote in awe.

Hewett would open new worlds to generations of students. As director of the School of American Research, he established field schools on the Pajarito Plateau where he and his students set to work systematically excavating the major sites in Frijoles Canyon and the surrounding area. His fervor was infectious. Hewett even acted as tour guide, escorting visitors personally through the sites.

The first site Hewett excavated was Tyuonyi, which would turn out to be one of the most impressive pueblo dwellings on the Pajarito Plateau. Viewed from above, Tyuonyi's nearly circular architectural plan is clear: its rooms were arranged in tiers of three to eight rooms that were two and sometimes three stories high, around a central outdoor plaza where most daily activity took place. At the plaza's north

A small, muscular man clad in a Spanish bolero jacket, corduroy trousers, a kerchief knotted rakishly around his head, Charles F. Lummis struck a colorful pose. At the camp along the Rito de los Frijoles he was already a giant among men. He had helped the *Los Angeles Times* grow into a major newspaper and served as its hard-driving city editor. Forced to retire from the newspaper life he loved because of a stroke that paralyzed his left side, he moved to New Mexico. He lived at Isleta Pueblo where he regained his health and wrote voluminously about the Southwest.

Born and raised in Massachusetts, the Harvard graduate was a newspaper man in Ohio when he set out in 1884, at age 25, to walk across the country—3,507 miles in 145 days—from Cincinnati across the

SOUTHWEST MUSEUM OF THE AMERICAN INDIAN

CHARLES F. LUMMIS

Southwest to the Pacific. After meeting Adolph Bandelier, he embarked on a new career as an amateur archeologist and ethnologist. The joy of those days with Bandelier in Frijoles Canyon shines through Lummis' writings: "Thousands of miles of wilderness and desert we trudged side by side, camped, starved, shivered, learned and were glad together. …Up and down pathless cliffs, through tangled canyons, fording icy streams and ankle-deep sands we traveled, no blankets, overcoats or other shelter and the only commissary a few cakes of sweet chocolate and small sack of parched pop-corn meal."

Later Lummis would be one of the founders of the School of American Research and friend to such great figures of Southwest archeology as Edgar Hewett and Frederick Hodge. He was friendly with the politicians and statesmen of this day, including President Theodore Roosevelt with whom he shared a great love for the wilderness of the West. The canyon just southwest of Frijoles Canyon was named for Charles F. Lummis.

end, and outside the pueblo to the east, are circular underground kivas with masonry walls.

The only ground-floor entrance to Tyuonyi was a narrow passageway on the east side. To enter a house at Tyuonyi, residents had to climb a ladder to the pueblo's second story and descend through a hatch in the roof. Like other canyon homesites, Tyuonyi was made from chunks of soft volcanic tuff. This soft stone did not fracture cleanly. Wall fragments show blocks of uneven size set into a

Dr. Edgar Lee Hewett excavated the dwelling in Frijoles Canyon in the first decade of the twenieth century, then moved on to other projects. The sites, with their protective layer of dirt removed, were then exposed to the elements for over twenty years. In the late 1930s, with funding and labor provided by the Civilian Conservation Corps, J.W. Hendron went to work re-excavating and stabilizing the dwellings. These careful drawings as seen during those re-excavations were done in 1930 by R.P. McClung for the Historic American Buildings Survey. The drawings reveal details no longer visible, such as the outlines on the rooms at the back of Alcove House.

thick mud mortar.

Tyuonyi's plaza is quiet and empty now, but five hundred years ago, it would have been alive with the sounds of human activity: mothers calling to their children, the sharp chipping of stone on stone as men chiseled their fine hunting points and other tools, the slower rhythms of corn being ground in stone basins, and turkeys squawking and scratching in the dust. At dusk many fires cast long, dark shadows against the walls. The small and smoky rooms, with no windows or doors to the outside, were unsuitable for most tasks, but offered security and relative comfort on bitter winter nights.

The other sites Hewett excavated are the multi-terraced masonry pueblos set against the base of the north cliffs. Not true cliff dwellings,

these structures were built against canyon walls, taking advantage of the many large fissures in the rock. Roof beams for rooms closest to the cliff wall rested in holes cut into the tuff. The builders burrowed into the cliff face to create additional rooms for living and storage, and in at least one instance, for a large ceremonial chamber.

Directly north of Tyuonyi are sites that Hewett called Sun House, Snake Village, and Cave Kiva. The first, named for the sun symbol pecked into the cliff face above it, contains some twenty-eight known rooms plus many more that have totally collapsed. Considerably larger, Snake Village includes an unusual cave kiva named for a feathered serpent painted on the plastered wall.

Cave Kiva is an oval ceremonial room cut out of the rock that measures nearly twenty feet across. Depressions in the floor and ceiling held support beams for two large looms used for weaving. These, along with the room's size, floor features, and smoke-blackened ceiling, indicate this room served as a kiva over a period of several generations. The National Park Service has restored part of this kiva and provides visitors access to it.

Long House, perhaps the canyon's most remarkable site, extends more than eight hundred feet along the cliff wall, beginning a quarter mile to the

Alcove House drawing by R.P. McClung, 1939

west of park headquarters. These large masonry dwellings had more than three hundred and fifty rooms arranged in rows from one-to-four rooms deep, with additional cave rooms dug into the cliff at the rear. The rooms were terraced up to three levels, as can be seen clearly from the neat rows of roof-beam sockets in the rock. Though most rooms have collapsed, some masonry wall fragments survive along with marks showing where rooms attached to the cliff face.

At various places in Long House, petroglyphs pecked into the cliff depict faces and human figures, serpents, and birds, including at least one macaw, a bird the ancestral Pueblo people imported from what is now Mexico. These rock art friezes may have graced the wall above dance plazas on the pueblo rooftops. Outdoor plazas play a similar role in modern pueblo life.

Hewett also undertook excavations at Alcove House, a spectacular natural cave situated one hundred and forty feet above the canyon floor west of Long House. The natural cave had been enlarged to provide clusters of living rooms accompanied by a small kiva. Today, visitors reach Alcove House by climbing one hundred and forty feet of ladders and stepping in the narrow footholds worn into the precipitous rock ledges.

About six miles from park headquarters by trail, lies the

Alcove House

large, mostly unexcavated site of Yapashi. The people who live at Cochiti Pueblo say their ancestors inhabited this village.

Five miles south of Yapashi sits Painted Cave, some thirty feet above the floor of Capulin Canyon. Generations of pueblo people, right up to the present, have climbed to this spectacular natural cave, using only a series of hand- and toe-holds in the north cliff face. On the cave's back wall, in tones of black, white, and red, are painted images important to the Pueblo world. They tell a fascinating story involving familiar animals as well as monster-like creatures,

human faces and kachina masks, and a man on horseback carrying a lance—obviously a Spanish soldier. Feathered serpents and sun spirals alongside a mission church and other Christian symbols line the cliff wall. Painted Cave remains a sacred place where respectful visitors, although forbidden from climbing into the cave, can experience a link with a link with an ongoing Pueblo culture.

Outside Frijoles Canyon, another large, mostly unexcavated pueblo lies within Bandelier. Tsankawi sits on the Pajarito Plateau at the edge of a finger-like mesa. Its fortress-like position offered great security but the inhabitants must also have enjoyed the view across the Rio Grande Valley to the Sangre de Cristo Mountains and back across the Pajarito to the Jemez. Like the homesites in the canyon, Tsankawi has both free-standing pueblo dwellings and cave homes dug into the cliff below.

This village adheres to a familiar plan with a central outdoor plaza containing two kivas. Several more kivas lie outside the perimeter. The villagers also built a reservoir on the edge of the mesa to collect precious rainfall. The path through the volcanic rock up to Tsankawi has been worn eighteen inches deep in some places by the passing of hundreds of human feet as the people traveled to and from the fields or toward their cliff homes. Today, when the morning sun glints off the rocks far below, the shadows of the past fall heavily across the trail, a haunting presence for all who climb up to this high, wind-swept village, silent now for centuries.

Archeologists learn about the lifeways of the past by examining

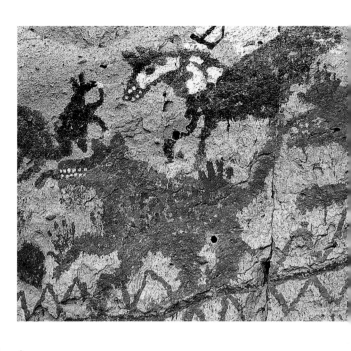

(OPPOSITE) **Painted Cave**

Detail of Painted Cave

Ancestral Pueblo trail at Tsankawi

Tall, graceful, and sculptured, Tsankawi Black-on-Cream is some of the finest Tewa pottery produced prior to the arrival of the Spanish colonists in 1598. The predominant design on the vessel represents the Awanya —the mythological giver of water and life. Jars like this were probably used for grain or water storage. You can see a prehistoric attempt to mend this jar—a crack just below the rim is held together by sinew wrapped through two mend holes.

(OPPOSITE) Tsankawi

objects found at a site: an arrow point, a piece of pottery, a feather or fragment of bone, snakes or stars etched into a wall. These physical odds-and-ends can yield theories about climate, diet, everyday activities, and ritual practices of the people who left them. If objects are removed from a site, the picture is distorted or may never be completed. Many sites are deliberately left as they are out of respect for the wishes of present-day Pueblo people, and in the hope that future scholars will find better, less destructive ways to study them.

As Hewett and other archeologists unearthed treasures, filling in the complex picture of ancestral Pueblo life with each new artifact, they competed with the relentless forces of wind, weather, and pothunters who plundered the unprotected sites. Ancient pottery, tools, and jewelry began to appear on the shelves of curio shops and in the homes of private collectors before scholars could record and preserve them for future study. Bandelier's work and writings, and the work of Hewett and others, had drawn wide attention to the archeological richness of the Pajarito Plateau. In 1902, the first attempt was made to preserve the fragile sites.

The proposed creation of "Cliff Cities National Park" would have preserved an area much larger than the present park, but it met powerful opposition from livestock and timber interests. For a while longer, these precious cultural and natural resources would be in jeopardy.

Edgar Hewett, not a man to let an irreplaceable resource slip through his fingers without a fight, took up the cause. He drafted guidelines that would protect antiquities located on federal lands and create preserves or parks around major sites. Hewett's views eventually prevailed, and in 1906 President Theodore Roosevelt signed the Antiquities Act, which empowered the president to proclaim as national monuments certain areas of historic or scientific interest. Ten years later, President Woodrow Wilson proclaimed Bandelier National

Monument, stating "Certain prehistoric aboriginal ruins. . . are of such unusual ethnologic, scientific, and educational interest. . . that the public interest would be promoted by preserving these relics of a vanished people with as much land as may be necessary for the proper protection thereof." The Forest Service managed the park until 1932 when the National Park Service took over its protection.

More than a century and a quarter have passed since the light on the cliffs caught Bandelier's eye. His vision of the continuity of life on the Pajarito Plateau and the patient work of Hewett and other early archeologists have been rewarded. The sites at Bandelier have enlarged our understanding of the past and the area's rich cultural heritage. Many facts about the life of the ancestral Pueblo people are now known: how tall they were and how long they lived, how they dressed, ate, worked, and fashioned beautiful objects out of clay and stone. More of the story lies in shadowy caves and rooms yet undiscovered and under mounds of earth that cover collapsed pueblo walls. The answers will be coaxed out by new generations of patient seekers. To walk the paths of Bandelier today is to feel a tangible kinship with the ancient people who inhabited so beautiful a world.

NATIONAL PARK SERVICE/SALLY KING

Petroglyph at Long House may represent a macaw, a bird prized for its bright feathers and obtained in trade from deep in Mexico.

NEW CANYON DWELLERS

News of Bandelier's many charms traveled fast. From the beginning of the twentieth century, people have been drawn to it in increasing numbers. Some have left a lasting mark.

In 1907, Judge A. Judson Abbot fell under the spell of Frijoles Canyon and built "The Ranch of the Ten Elders" alongside the sparkling creek. The ranch buildings were later leased by John E. Davenport and in 1925, Evelyn and George Frey formed a partnership with him for the "business of conducting a hotel and resort in Frijoles Canyon." A few years later, the Freys became concessioners and negotiated a lease with the U.S. Forest Service to run "Frijoles Canyon Ranch."

The Freys and their guests carted all their goods down into the canyon on horseback along a half-mile set of switchbacks known today as the "Frey Trail." Near the creek, Evelyn cultivated a small orchard, which still bears fruit. George built an ingenious cable and basket system to haul supplies and baggage over the cliff, including a Dodge truck that had to be completely dismantled and later reassembled for carrying supplies around the canyon. The canyon's beauty and the Freys' fame as innkeepers drew increasing numbers of visitors to

CONSTRUCTING NATIONAL MONUMENT HOTEL

NATIONAL PARKS SERVICE

Bandelier's natural wonders.

During the Depression in 1933, a federal employment program, the Civilian Conservation Corps (CCC), was put to work in many national parks and on other Federal lands. Frijoles Canyon witnessed a building boom, the first in six hundred years! The sound of the stonemason's hammer once again reverberated off canyon walls, but now noisy compressors and cement mixers added to the din. After building the first road into the canyon, the CCC constructed a handsome group of park buildings: a visitor center, a new guest lodge to replace the Freys' successful ranch, a dining room, coffee shop, gift shop, and staff quarters. These buildings,

constructed of the same type of stone the ancestral Pueblo people used centuries earlier, echoed the shape and style of the ancient buildings farther up the canyon. The Depression-era work at Bandelier wasn't all muscle. The Works Progress Administration also commissioned two artists, Pueblo painter Pablita Velarde and pastelist Helmut Naumer, to create works for the visitor center.

CCC craftsmen fashioned tables and chairs, even curtain rods, and fashioned intricate, pierced-tin chandeliers and wall sconces. Examples of the wood carvings and chandeliers can be seen in the visitor center. These thirty-one stone structures, the largest surviving group of CCC-

Depression-era work programs created much-needed visitor facilities in many National Park areas, including Bandelier National Monument. The Civilian Conservation Corps (CCC) provided jobs for young men throughout the country. Enrollees worked hard, learned skills, and earned their room and board plus one dollar a day. Between 1933 and 1940, crews at Bandelier built the entrance road and trails through the dwellings and the backcountry. The visitor center and Frijoles Canyon Lodge were designed to blend with the landscape. The complex they built is the largest collection of CCC buildings in any National Park Service area in the country, and in 1987 the Bandelier CCC Historic District was designated a National Historic Landmark.

era buildings in any National Park Service area, are constantly being refurbished and restored. In 1987, they were designated a Historic District in the National Historic Landmark Program and placed on the National Register of Historic Places. Visitors can no longer stay overnight at the park lodge, but they can still enjoy the sight of these beautiful park buildings.

The war years ushered in another interesting chapter in Bandelier's history: The government was suddenly acquiring the lands of ranchers on the surrounding plateau. Mrs. Frey was told to close her lodge to all but those who were involved in the supper-secret Manhattan Project. It wasn't until 1945 when the world learned that the new guests at Frijoles Canyon Lodge were working to develop an atomic bomb.

After the war, the Pajarito Plateau again bustled with activity. Many of those who had come to work on the Manhattan Project grew to love the beautiful canyon and mesa country and decided to stay. Mrs. Frey continued to run the guest lodge, which remained open until 1976 when it closed permanently, and the buildings went back to the government for use by the National park Service.

In 1987, the National Park Service began a new archeological survey of many of the major sites within Bandelier. The study was designed to take four years of fieldwork followed by three years of analysis and writing. In its first summer, archeologists recorded 467 sites, ranging from small shrines and storage rooms to hundred-room pueblos. Archeologists now know there are more than 3,000 separate sites within the park. These sites will certainly tell more about

NATIONAL PARK SERVICE

EVELYN FREY

In 1929, before there was a road into Frijoles Canyon, thirty-two-hundred visitors nonetheless made their way down the precipitous trail to explore Bandelier National Monument and to enjoy the hospitality of Evelyn Frey. On December 9, 1933, when the first automobile drove down the newly completed road into the canyon, Evelyn Frey was its first passenger. By then, her reputation as a gracious hostess and unofficial guide to Bandelier was widely known. It was said she treated everyone alike, from ambassadors and New York financiers to shopkeepers from nearby Santa Fe.

When the new Civilian Conservation Corps lodge buildings were erected in the 1930s, no detail was too small to receive Mrs. Frey's attention. She saw that the wild-turkey motif that was carved into the handmade furniture was carried throughout the building—it even decorated the lodge dinnerware. She ran, what was described as "the most wonderful dining room," serving food that, in itself, was worth the trip to the canyon. After the lodge closed, Mrs. Frey continued to live in Frijoles Canyon, working summers at the visitor center until her death in 1988 when she was in her mid nineties. For more than half a century, she shared her love for Bandelier and the knowledge gathered over a lifetime with park visitors.

the ancestral Pueblo people who lived here between 1150 CE and 1600 CE and provide new clues to explain why they moved away. The sunlit villages at the bottom of Frijoles Canyon and shadowy cave dwellings along its walls are just a fragment of the whole, a vast network of villages and homesites which once filled the Pajarito Plateau with life.

NATIONAL PARK SERVICE

PABILTA VELARDE

In 1939, a shy, nineteen-year-old woman was invited to paint a series of historical panels for the National Park Service at Bandelier National Monument. Pablita Velarde was embarking on a brave new career path for women of her culture. Golden Dawn, the Tewa name given to her by her grandmother, roamed the mesas and canyons of Pajarito Plateau as a child, helping her widowed father farm and playing with her sister in the cave dwellings carved into the sheer cliffs. Their afternoons were filled with discoveries: painted potsherds, fantastic figures chipped into the rock, fragments of murals painted on cave walls. She stored all of these images in her mind along with the daily rituals of pueblo life.

She spent several years at St. Catherine's Indian School in Sante Fe where the nuns named her "Pablita" and where she learned English. Later, at the Santa Fe Indian School, her talent developed, nurtured by encouraging teachers. But Pablita returned often to the wellspring of her creativity, her home at Santa Clara Pueblo. Like pueblos all along the Rio Grande Valley, its buildings echo the shapes of the buttes and mesas that surround it. The pastel colors and flat roofs with ladders connecting the worlds of light and dark recall those built so long ago in Bandelier.

Until she passed away in 2006, Pablita produced her prized "earth paintings," returning to the canyons of Santa Clara to collect rocks for grinding into natural pigments on her grinding stone. When the stones were ground to a fine powder, she carefully funneled the colored dust into jars that line her studio like a captured rainbow. For inspiration she remembered the stories told to her as a child: "They are not legends to me," she said. "They are real." In the exquisite detail and symbolism of Pablita's "memory paintings" of pueblo life, the ancient and modern worlds meet.

WILDERNESS REFUGE

Bandelier National Monument's human and natural histories are inseparable. Its early dwellers saw its streams, vegetation, and wildlife as vital resources for survival in an otherwise harsh environment. And they cannot have been immune to its beauty.

Today, more than 10,000 years after its first visitors appeared, Bandelier attracts more than 300,000 people each year. Bandelier's allure is unchanged. It is still a bountiful area of transforming power and beauty.

Twenty-three thousand acres, some two-thirds of the park, have been designated a wilderness area, and today's park visitors increasingly come for the joy of experiencing this pristine environment. They arrive at the park entrance by car and van and on foot, their eyes fixed on the winding road and spectacular cliffs ahead. They may be unaware that the steep descent from mesa top to canyon bottom—some 400 vertical feet—holds the secret to Bandelier's uniqueness as a wilderness experience.

The range in elevation is the reason for the diversity of terrain and life forms that has made the Pajarito such a haven for human activity. The ancestral Pueblo people used the plants and animals that can survive in warm, dry conditions at low elevations as well as those which flourish in a cooler, wetter climate at higher elevations.

In White Rock Canyon, where Frijoles Creek meets the Rio Grande after tumbling over two major falls, high-desert plants such as cactus, sagebrush, and juniper thrive. Lush riparian vegetation grows all along Frijoles Creek and is especially enjoyed by walkers and picnickers near the visitor center. Here waterbirch, box elder, and narrowleaf cottonwood lean over the year-round stream fed by springs, snow melt, and summer rains. Most of these trees lose their leaves in the fall to provide a thick, fertile compost that naturally replenishes soil nutrients.

The same streamside shrubbery provides a habitat for many small animals: raccoons, the tassel-eared Abert's squirrel, wood rats, and other small mammals that in turn attract their natural predators: coyote, fox, mountain lion, and bobcat. These larger animals range freely up and down the canyon's vegetation zones searching for food.

The thick, tangled growth along the creek also houses a variety of small birds, as do the grapevines, which drape willows and cottonwoods near the Rio Grande. Songbirds fill the summer canyon air: black-headed grosbeak, hermit thrush, western tanager, and warblers, their notes all topped by the sweet, high trill of the canyon wren. An occasional flash of orange signals a flicker about to drum on the bark of a tree, hunting for insects. Flycatchers, swallows, and swifts snatch their insect meals from midair.

The Rio Grande is a major flyway for migrating waterfowl, songbirds, raptors, and Sandhill cranes. Ducks,

(OPPOSITE) **El Rito de los Frijoles**

Mule Deer

geese, and shorebirds traverse this busy thoroughfare. Eagles winter here and feed on fish and ducks. The 1987 archeological survey recorded the presence of several deep pits dug down into the rock on top of the mesas. It is believed these were used to trap eagles and hawks which the ancestral Pueblo people may have used in their ceremonies.

In winter, flocks of wild turkeys move from nesting sites high in the Jemez Mountains to the canyon bottom where they feed on acorns, nuts, and juniper berries. The ancestral Pueblo people built turkey pens near their homesites and wove turkey feathers and yucca fibers to make blankets to ward off winter's chill.

Some summers a colony of more than ten thousand Mexican free-tailed bats live in a cave directly above Long House. In those summers, each evening these nocturnal mammals fly out to hunt insects and return to their cave before dawn. The bats raise their young in the canyon, then migrate south for the winter. A dozen species of bats are known to live in Bandelier.

Higher up the slope at the base of the cliffs and climbing toward the mesas, pinon and juniper woodlands predominate with a scattering of ponderosa pine and scrub oak. This vegetation group characterizes about half of Bandelier's total area. The soil in the piñon-juniper forest tends to be thin and erodes easily, a problem worsened by heavy livestock grazing

Piñon-juniper woodlands

From the earliest sites in the Bandelier area to the modern Pueblos along the Rio Grande Valley, small animal figurines have been modeled from clay. Compare the skunk (top), that was made at Cochiti Pueblo in the 1970s and the figure made at a village in the Bandelier area about 800 years ago.

(OPPOSITE) Wildflower display in the conifer forest: dotted gayfeather (purple), bitterweed (yellow), scarlet gilia (red)

Spruce-fir uplands

in the nineteenth century. Wild burros that roamed freely also greatly reduced the ground cover. Piñon-juniper woodlands are still home to many cottontail rabbits, squirrels, and piñon mice.

Ascending into the Jemez foothills 8,000 feet and above, piñon, juniper, and ponderosa pine give way to quaking aspen and a mixed conifer forest of spruce, white fir and Douglas fir. These tall trees shelter delicate ground cover and moisture-loving grasses. Elk, black bear, and mountain lion roam here. Bears are more likely to be seen along the creek in summer. The elk travel up to ten miles to find a warm, protected site at calving time. Mountain lions are rarely seen.

A patient observer may see some of the park's most common inhabitants, such as mule deer, gray-headed junco, and eastern fence lizard. Others like the Jemez Mountain salamander, a rare creature on the state's endangered species list, have

been spotted only at certain altitudes and even on specific slopes.

The highest point in the park is the 10,199-foot peak of Cerro Grande, once covered by ancient montane grasslands. Today, because of modern fire suppression, spruce, fir, and pine have invaded the grasslands and changed native habitats.

Visitors to Bandelier are often treated to glorious wildflower displays. More than nine hundred individual plant species have been recorded throughout the park. In spring, Indian paintbrush and perky sue present their showy blooms. In summer, the walking-stick cholla and, the hummingbirds' favorite, red penstemon brighten the piñon-juniper woodlands and bottomlands. In fall, golden chamisa lavishly line every trail and roadway, and Virginia creeper turns pale stone walls to crimson. Bandelier is also home to some very rare species, including the golden lady-slipper.

On a map, Bandelier appears as the comfortably placed center of a much larger natural area. A closer look reveals that there is increasing human activity outside the park boundary and no buffer zone to insulate it from the outside world. Each year more and more people, using more and more of the surrounding land, exert increasing pressure on Bandelier.

Logging, mineral extraction,

housing and business development, and expanding government research all threaten the park.

Bandelier is as complex and ephemeral as a spider's web: when any portion of it is touched, the whole intricate fabric trembles. Preservation of Bandelier's natural

Yapashi

environment, from its scenic views to its fragile and diverse ecosystem, will entail a struggle with the larger world in which it exists.

The construction of Cochiti Dam downstream from Frijoles Canyon, for example, dramatically altered the water levels of a once-beautiful part of the park. Flooding from the dam occasionally raises water levels as much as one hundred feet above the former river surface, producing a kind of bathtub ring of sediment and debris. The dam has made

one of the park's most popular backcountry trails unusable, destroyed natural vegetation, and altered the balance of nature in this part of the park.

Many species of animals have already been crowded out of Bandelier. The grizzly bear, bighorn sheep, and the wolf, once fairly common here, no longer roam the mesas. The river otter is no longer found in the clear, cold streams.

Changes in the pattern of tree and plant life may not seem obvious to the untrained eye, but they are potentially destructive and long lasting. On the highest Jemez peaks, people once waded through large stretches of montane grasslands, thousands of years old. These grasslands were a diverse habitat for many plants and animals. Swaying in waves before the wind, the tall grasses were a beautiful and essential aspect of the landscape. They kept the rich mountain soil from blowing and washing away. In their place today, spruce and fir stand out against the sky. These trees are beautiful, too, but they are intruders in what was grassland habitat and present a problem for park management.

The loss of grassland is also apparent in the piñon-juniper woodlands. The dense, fibrous root system of grasses stabilizes the soil of the lower mesa areas more effectively than the wide-spreading piñon and juniper roots. When the grasses die, erosion accelerates. Small tree roots quickly become exposed to the elements, and in many places in the park they can be seen as grotesque pedestals, with the tree barely clinging to life. Wind, rain, and frost, allowed to work without restraint on the surface soil, are eroding more than thirty-two tons of soil per acre per year. Erosion also threatens the irreplaceable archeological resources within the piñon-juniper woodland. It will take generations of painstaking work at great expense to replenish the soil and regenerate these grasslands.

Ground cover and grasses were also a perfect conduit for the healthy, cleansing fires that would periodically race across the mesas, reducing the density of competing trees and bushes. For centuries fire has been a frequent and natural visitor to Bandelier as it is to many wilderness areas. Most people think of fire as a threat, which ought to be stopped at all costs. Images of Smokey Bear and Bambi have been all too effective in convincing us of the need for total fire suppression. In reality, studies show that fires started by lightning have always been an important element in maintaining the balance of Bandelier's ecosystem. These were "cool," cleansing fires, which generally burned along the floors of mixed conifer and pine forests. Fueled by young shoots, grasses, bushes, fallen limbs and leaves, such fires burned across the park on average once every ten years before the policy of fire suppression was instituted in the early twentieth century.

After 1910, every time a puff

of smoke was spotted, people and machines moved quickly to extinguish it. The policy seemed good in the short run, but spelled disaster for the long-term health of the forest. Left unchecked, forests in Bandelier and across the West have grown denser, and potentially burnable materials, called fuel loads, have accumulated to dangerous levels. As fire suppression decreased the total number of fires, the intensity of those that did break out increased. Even the nature of fire has changed with man's intervention. Today's fires are more commonly the highly destructive crown fires that leap from one treetop to another, not the more natural and beneficial ground fires. Fire suppression simply postpones the inevitable. One day lightning may strike or an unextinguished campfire may ignite those fuel loads.

That fate visited Bandelier in 1977 when La Mesa Fire raged out of control. Before it was suppressed, it burned more than 14,000 acres, including roughly one-third of the park. The effects of the fire are clearly visible along the park boundary on New Mexico Highway 4. In that fire's wake, growth is also visible. Although La Mesa Fire was an intense and catastrophic blaze, it still provided the landscape with an opportunity for restoration.

Another significant crown fire, the 1996 Dome Fire, consumed 16,000 acres, 4,000 in the park. Though blackened trees are still

Piñon mouse

Indian paintbrush and tall grass of the plateau

visible, as with La Mesa Fire, the fire released nutrients into the soil and stimulated many fire-resistant seeds to germinate, bringing an explosion of growth. With the flourishing vegetation, wildlife populations rebounded.

By contrast, resource managers called the 1997 Lummis Fire a "prescribed natural fire." Ignited by a lightning strike, it burned more slowly than the explosive blazes of the Dome and La Mesa fires. The 1,000-acre Lummis Fire crept across the ground, burning mostly grasses, brush, and dead and downed logs. Two decades earlier, the La Mesa Fire had cleared the area of shrubs and small trees, preventing an intense, destructive blaze. The Lummis Fire continued the cycle, insuring several more years of "prescribed" rejuvenation for the terrain.

That was not the case in 2000. A prescribed fire, lit by Bandelier National Monument to reduce fuel loads and the risk of large wildfires, burned out of control. The Cerro Grande Fire, driven by 60-mph winds, exploded across 43,000 acres and destroyed the homes of more than 400 families in nearby Los Alamos. Recovery for the forest and the community is slow, but progressing.

Management of Bandelier's fragile ecosystem grows more complex and difficult each year. Its very popularity as a wilderness area can be a threat to its survival. Hundreds of thousands of visitors a year walk the park trails. The park's excavated archeological sites lie exposed to wind and rain and to potential damage by humans. Thousands of unexcavated sites are vulnerable, too, and it is important they remain undisturbed out of respect for their Pueblo descendents and for further study. The wilderness world of Bandelier, most fragile of all, requires constant vigilance so that future generations can experience this landscape.

BANDELIER'S ENDURING MAGIC

Since that bright October day when Adolph Bandelier followed his Cochiti guide down the steep trail to Frijoles Canyon, millions of visitors have come to appreciate the restorative powers of Bandelier's natural beauty and to learn about its ancient peoples. How long this precious resource for study, quiet contemplation, and wilderness adventure remains depends on the commitment to preserve and protect it.

Management at Bandelier continues the work of those who came before, including the ancestral Pueblo people, Evelyn Frey, Adolph Bandelier, Charles Lummis, Edgar Hewett, Pablita Velarde, and Helmuth Naumer. Today, the National Park Service and the Pueblo people are leaders in the effort to ensure that the world of Bandelier, a world of "ineffable light and sudden shadows," will survive and continue to draw us under its spell.

(OPPOSITE) **Reminders of the La Mesa Fire of 1977**

Bandelier Black-on-Gray is often called "biscuit ware" by archeologists because of the resemblance of this pottery to china in the bisque phase of manufacture. The bowls were common from Frijoles Canyon north to the Ojo Caliente area during the Rio Grande Classic period and are characterized by thick walls and black paint applied on a gray or tan surface. These bowls were probably used for serving food.

FURTHER READING

Bandelier, Adolph. *The Delight Makers,* A Harvest Book, 1971.

Gustafson, Sarah. *Pecos National Historical Park,* Western National Parks Association, 2009.

Lamb, Susan. *Petroglyph National Monument,* Western National Parks Association, 2005.

Lister, Robert H. and Florence C. Lister. *Those Who Came Before,* Western National Parks Association, 1993.

Strutin, Michele. *Chaco: A Cultural Legacy,* Western National Parks Association, 1994.

Thybony, Scott. *Aztec Ruins National Monument,* Western National Parks Association, 1992.

OTHER PLACES TO VISIT

Aztec Ruins National Monument
Coronado State Monument
Chaco Culture National Historical Park
Mesa Verde National Park
Jemez State Monument
Pecos National Historical Park
Petroglyph National Monument
Salinas Pueblo Missions National Monument

Lower Falls in Frijoles Canyon